TOP 10 MOMENTS IN BASEBALL

By Nathan Sommer

Minneapolis, Minnesota

Credits

Cover and title page, © Tribune Content Agency LLC/Alamy Stock Photo and EmiLL/peopleimages.com/Adobe Stock and noraismail/Adobe Stock; 4, © tammykayphoto/Adobe Stock and © 103tnn/Adobe Stock and © Yuri Arcurs/peopleimages.com/Adobe Stock and © J Bettencourt/peopleimages.com/Adobe Stock and © Lumeez Ismail/peopleimages.com/Adobe Stock and © Debra Lawrence/Adobe Stock and © slocummedia/Adobe Stock and © steven hendricks/Adobe Stock and © kirkikis/Adobe Stock and © soupstock/Adobe Stock and © Iris Nieves/Adobe Stock and © Don Mroczkowski /Adobe Stock and © Joe/Adobe Stock and © Artur Didyk/Adobe Stock and © Taira Masao/Adobe Stock and © cfarmer/Adobe Stock and © magdal3na/Adobe Stock and © moodboard/Adobe Stock and © Mike Watson Images Limited/Adobe Stock and © edojob/Adobe Stock and © Philip/Adobe Stock; 5, © NY Daily News/Getty Images; 6, © Megan Briggs/Getty Images; 6–7, © Kyodo/Associated Press; 8, © MLB Photos/Getty Images; 8–9, © Heinz Kluetmeier/Getty Images; 10–11, © Chuck Solomon/Getty Images; 12, © John Iacono/Getty Images; 13, © Bettmann Archive/Getty Images; 14–15, © MIKE FIALA/Getty Images; 16, © Tribune Content Agency LLC /Alamy Stock Photo; 16–17,© Aflo Co. Ltd./Alamy Stock Photo; 18,© Ron Vesely/Getty Images; 19, © Focus On Sport/Getty Images; 20–21, © Sporting News Archive/Getty Images; 22TR, © Bettmann Archive/Getty Images; 22ML, © John Iacono/Getty Images; 22BR, © Bryan Yablonsky/Sportschrome/Getty Images; 23BR, © BillionPhotos/Adobe Stock

Bearport Publishing Company Product Development Team

Publisher: Jen Jenson; Director of Product Development: Spencer Brinker; Editorial Director: Allison Juda; Editor: Cole Nelson; Editor: Tiana Tran; Production Editor: Naomi Reich; Art Director: Kim Jones; Designer: Kayla Eggert; Designer: Steve Scheluchin; Production Specialist: Owen Hamlin

Statement on Usage of Generative Artificial Intelligence

Bearport Publishing remains committed to publishing high-quality nonfiction books. Therefore, we restrict the use of generative AI to ensure accuracy of all text and visual components pertaining to a book's subject. See BearportPublishing.com for details.

Library of Congress Cataloging-in-Publication Data

Names: Sommer, Nathan, author.
Title: Top 10 moments in baseball / by Nathan Sommer.
Other titles: Top ten moments in baseball
Description: Minneapolis, Minnesota : Bearport Publishing Company, 2026. | Series: Top 10 sports extremes | Includes bibliographical references and index.
Identifiers: LCCN 2025001544 (print) | LCCN 2025001545 (ebook) | ISBN 9798895770610 (library binding) | ISBN 9798895775080 (paperback) | ISBN 9798895771785 (ebook)
Subjects: LCSH: Baseball--History--Juvenile literature.
Classification: LCC GV867.5 .S653 2026 (print) | LCC GV867.5 (ebook) | DDC 796.35709--dc23/eng/20250213
LC record available at https://lccn.loc.gov/2025001544
LC ebook record available at https://lccn.loc.gov/2025001545

Copyright © 2026 Bearport Publishing Company. All rights reserved. No part of this publication may be reproduced in whole or in part, stored in any retrieval system, or transmitted in any form or by any means, electronic, mechanical, photocopying, recording, or otherwise, without written permission from the publisher. Bearport Publishing is a division of FlutterBee Education Group.

For more information, write to Bearport Publishing, 3500 American Blvd W, Suite 150, Bloomington, MN 55431.

CONTENTS

America's Favorite Pastime 4
#10 The Catch 5
#9 A Friendly Face-off 6
#8 Saving the Day 8
#7 Steal of the Century 10
#6 Gibson's Walk-Off 12
#5 Breaking Records 13
#4 Rise of the Underdogs 14
#3 Breaking the Curse 16
#2 Joe Carter's Game Winner 18
#1 Shot Heard 'Round the World 20

Even More Extreme Baseball Moments 22
Glossary 23
Index 24
Read More 24
Learn More Online 24
About the Author 24

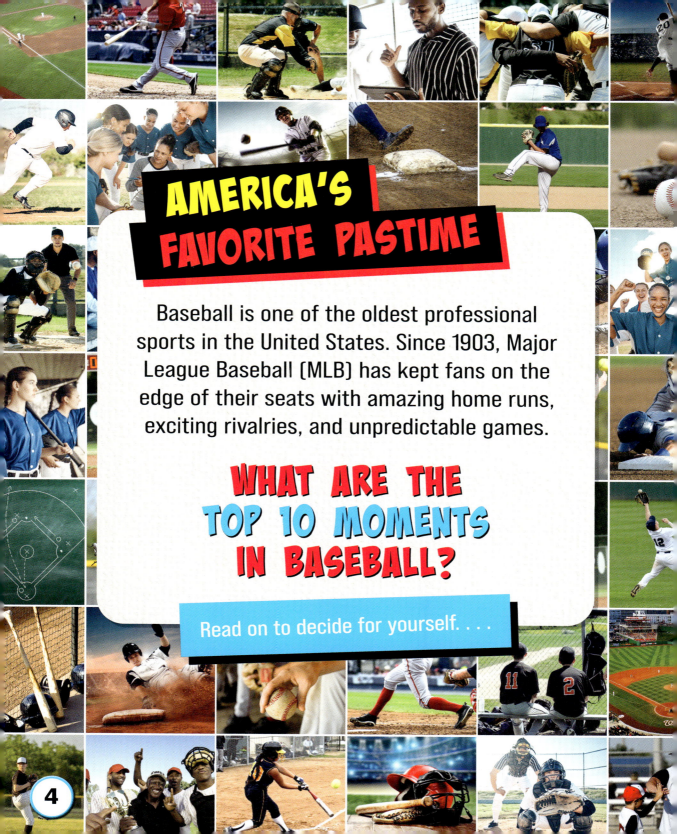

AMERICA'S FAVORITE PASTIME

Baseball is one of the oldest professional sports in the United States. Since 1903, Major League Baseball (MLB) has kept fans on the edge of their seats with amazing home runs, exciting rivalries, and unpredictable games.

WHAT ARE THE TOP 10 MOMENTS IN BASEBALL?

Read on to decide for yourself. . . .

#10 THE CATCH

September 29, 1954 ▪ Polo Grounds ▪ New York City, New York

The New York Giants and Cleveland Guardians (at the time known as the Indians) were tied 2–2 in the 8th inning of Game 1 of the 1954 World Series. But then, Cleveland batter Vic Wertz cracked a **fly ball** deep into center field. It looked like Cleveland was about to score. However, Giants center fielder Willie Mays caught the ball over his shoulder—while still running!

This catch is considered one of the best defensive plays in MLB history.

Mays was an MLB All-Star 24 times!

The Giants would go on to win the 1954 World Series.

5

#9 A FRIENDLY FACE-OFF

March 21, 2023 • LoanDepot Park • Miami, Florida

At the top of the 9th inning of the 2023 World Baseball Classic Championship, Japan led the United States 3–2. Japan pitcher Shohei Ohtani faced off against Mike Trout, his MLB teammate from the Los Angeles Angels. Ohtani struck out Trout on a **full count**. The game ended with Japan as the victors!

The game clinched Japan's third championship win.

Ohtani (*center right*) celebrates with his teammates.

This was one of the most-watched baseball games ever.

Japan had an undefeated record for the 2023 tournament.

Ohtani was named MVP of the 2023 World Baseball Classic.

7

#8 SAVING THE DAY

October 26, 1991 • Hubert H. Humphrey Metrodome
Minneapolis, Minnesota

The Minnesota Twins and Atlanta Braves were tied during Game 6 of the 1991 World Series. A Twins loss would have put an end to the series. But then, Kirby Puckett of the Twins stepped up to the plate in the 11th inning. He hit a **walk-off** home run into left field to force a Game 7!

This series became the Twins' third championship win.

In this series, five of the seven games were decided by a single run.

Earlier in Game 6, Puckett made a leaping catch to stop a home run.

The Twins became the first team to win an MLB championship after finishing in last place the previous year.

Puckett hit 207 home runs in his career.

#7 STEAL OF THE CENTURY

October 17, 2004 • Fenway Park • Boston, Massachusetts

It was a tense matchup during Game 4 of the 2004 American League Championship between the Boston Red Sox and the New York Yankees. The top of the ninth inning found the Red Sox behind by one run. Then, Red Sox player Dave Roberts **stole** second and scored on a single run. The play forced extra innings, leading to a 6–4 Red Sox victory.

The only season Roberts played for the Red Sox was 2004.

Roberts steals second base.

The Red Sox went on to win the 2004 championship series.

This game led to the Red Sox's first championship win in 86 years.

The Red Sox are the only team to come back after trailing a series 3–0.

#6 GIBSON'S WALK-OFF

October 15, 1988 • Dodger Stadium • Los Angeles, California

During the 1988 World Series, Los Angeles Dodgers player Kirk Gibson was held out of Game 1 with leg injuries. Then, as the Dodgers trailed the Oakland Athletics 4–3, Gibson was called in to **pinch hit**. With the team already two outs down, Gibson hit a walk-off homer, scoring two runs! The Dodgers won 5–4.

This was Gibson's only time batting during the entire World Series.

Before batting, Gibson watched most of the game in the Dodgers' **clubhouse**.

The Dodgers would go on to win the 1988 World Series in five games.

Gibson (*left*) cheered on by his coach, Manny Mota (*right*)

#5 BREAKING RECORDS

April 8, 1974 ▪ Atlanta-Fulton County Stadium ▪ Atlanta, Georgia

On April 8, 1974, Atlanta Braves player Hank Aaron hit a home run. But this was not just any home run. . . . It was the 715th of Aaron's career! Aaron had just broken Babe Ruth's record that had held strong for 39 years. It was a record many people thought would live on forever.

Aaron was an All-Star 25 times. This is the most of any player in MLB history.

Aaron holds the record for most career **runs batted in** with 2,297.

Aaron hit a total of 755 home runs in his career.

#4 RISE OF THE UNDERDOGS

November 4, 2001 • Bank One Ballpark • Phoenix, Arizona

The Yankees entered the 2001 World Series as favorites against the Arizona Diamondbacks. Before Game 6, they led 3–2. But in the next game, the Diamondbacks **blew out** the Yankees 15–2, forcing a Game 7. Again, the Yankees had a chance. They were up 2-1 in the final inning of Game 7. That is, until Diamondback Luis Gonzalez hit a single to score two runs. The underdogs won!

This was the first time the Diamondbacks played in the World Series.

At the time, the Diamondbacks had been a team for only four years.

The Yankees had won the previous three World Series.

Every game in this series was won by the home team.

#3 BREAKING THE CURSE

November 2, 2016 ▪ Progressive Field ▪ Cleveland, Ohio

Beginning in 1945, the Chicago Cubs experienced an unlucky streak called the Curse of the Billy Goat. Things didn't turn around for them until 2016's World Series against the Cleveland Guardians. After 9 innings, the game was tied 6–6. The Cubs took control in the 10th inning and won with a final score of 8–7. The curse was finally broken!

What started the curse? Supposedly, a fan showed up with his pet goat and was asked to leave.

In 2016, the Cubs won 103 games—their most wins since 1910.

The win ended the longest championship **drought** in American sports history.

This was also the first time the Cubs had played in the World Series since 1945.

#2 JOE CARTER'S GAME WINNER

October 23, 1993 ▪ SkyDome ▪ Toronto, Ontario

In Game 6 of the 1993 World Series, the Toronto Blue Jays led the Philadelphia Phillies 5–1. Then, the Phillies scored five runs in a row. They entered the 9th inning with a 6–5 lead. But in the bottom of the 9th, Joe Carter hit a walk-off 3-run homer, and the Blue Jays won their second championship!

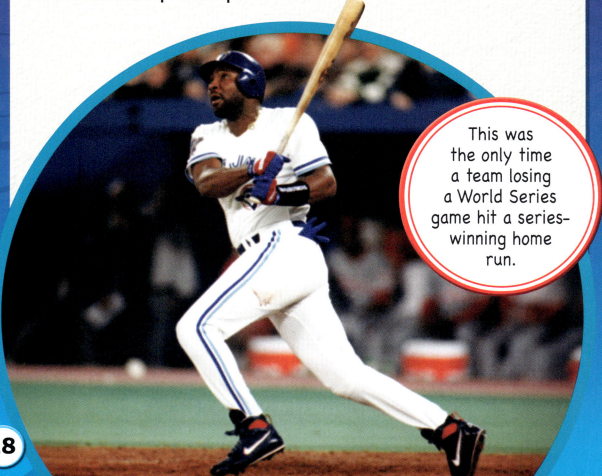

This was the only time a team losing a World Series game hit a series-winning home run.

#1 SHOT HEARD 'ROUND THE WORLD

October 3, 1951 • Polo Grounds • New York City, New York

The New York Giants and Brooklyn Dodgers faced off for 1951's National League **pennant**. Trailing 4–2 in the 9th inning, Giants player Bobby Thomson stepped up to the plate with two runners on base. After one strike, Thomson hit a home run deep into left field! The 3-run score allowed for a 5–4 comeback.

Thomson batted in four of the five runs the Giants scored during the game.

Thomson hits a home run into left field (*ball path highlighted in yellow*).

Thomson hit 20 home runs or more in each of the 8 seasons of his career.

20

Each team entered the game with a 96–58 record.

During the 1951 season, Thomson hit a career-high 32 home runs.

The Giants lost the 1951 World Series to the New York Yankees.

21

EVEN MORE EXTREME BASEBALL MOMENTS

Professional baseball has created many memories for fans over the years. Here are some other exciting top moments in baseball history.

THE PERFECT GAME
New York Yankees's Don Larsen pitched a **perfect game** during Game 5 of the 1956 World Series. This is the only perfect game in World Series history.

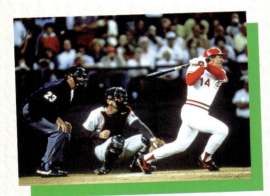

ANOTHER HIT!
On September 11, 1985, Cincinnati Reds player Pete Rose recorded his 4,192nd career hit. He broke Ty Cobb's record for most hits in MLB history!

A RECORD-BREAKING GAME
Cal Ripken Jr. of the Baltimore Orioles played his 2,131st game in a row on September 6, 1995. He broke the record for most consecutive games played.

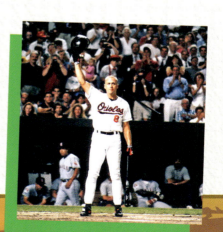

GLOSSARY

blew out won a game by many points

clubhouse an area at a ballpark that contains a team's locker room, gym, and doctor's office

drought a long period of time in which a team does not win a championship

fly ball a batted ball that travels high through the air rather than rolling along the ground

full count a play where a batter has two strikes and three balls leading into a pitch

pennant the championship of a league

perfect game a performance where a pitcher goes the entire game without allowing a batter on base

pinch hit to replace another batter in the lineup

runs batted in hits that allow runs to be scored

stole when a runner on base advances to the next base without a ball being hit

walk-off a winning run that ends the game

INDEX

bases 10, 14, 20
batter 5
catch 5, 9
home run 4, 8–9, 13, 18–21
MLB 4–6, 9, 13, 22
MVP 7
out 6, 12
pitcher 6
player 8, 10, 12–13, 19–20, 22
record 7, 13, 21–22
strike 20
teammate 6
World Series 5, 8, 12, 14–19, 22

READ MORE

Berglund, Bruce. *Baseball Records Smashed! (Sports Illustrated Kids: Record Smashers).* North Mankato, MN: Capstone Press, 2024.

Borden, Dani. *Baseball's Biggest Rivalries (Sports Illustrated Kids: Great Sports Rivalries).* North Mankato, MN: Capstone Press, 2024.

Streeter, Anthony. *World Series All-Time Greats (All-Time Greats of Sports Championships).* Mendota Heights, MN: Press Box Books, 2025.

LEARN MORE ONLINE

1. Go to **FactSurfer.com** or scan the QR code below.
2. Enter "**10 Baseball Moments**" into the search box.
3. Click on the cover of this book to see a list of websites.

ABOUT THE AUTHOR

Nathan Sommer graduated from the University of Minnesota with degrees in journalism and political science. He lives in Minneapolis, Minnesota, and enjoys camping, hiking, and writing in his free time.